100 FIRST WORDS BOOK

Children's Reading & Writing Education Books

SPEEDY
PUBLISHING

Speedy Publishing LLC
40 E. Main St. #1156
Newark, DE 19711
www.speedypublishing.com

Copyright 2016

All Rights reserved. No part of this book may be reproduced or used in any way or form or by any means whether electronic or mechanical, this means that you cannot record or photocopy any material ideas or tips that are provided in this book

TRACE, WRITE and READ.

Trace the word.

Write the word.

Read the word.

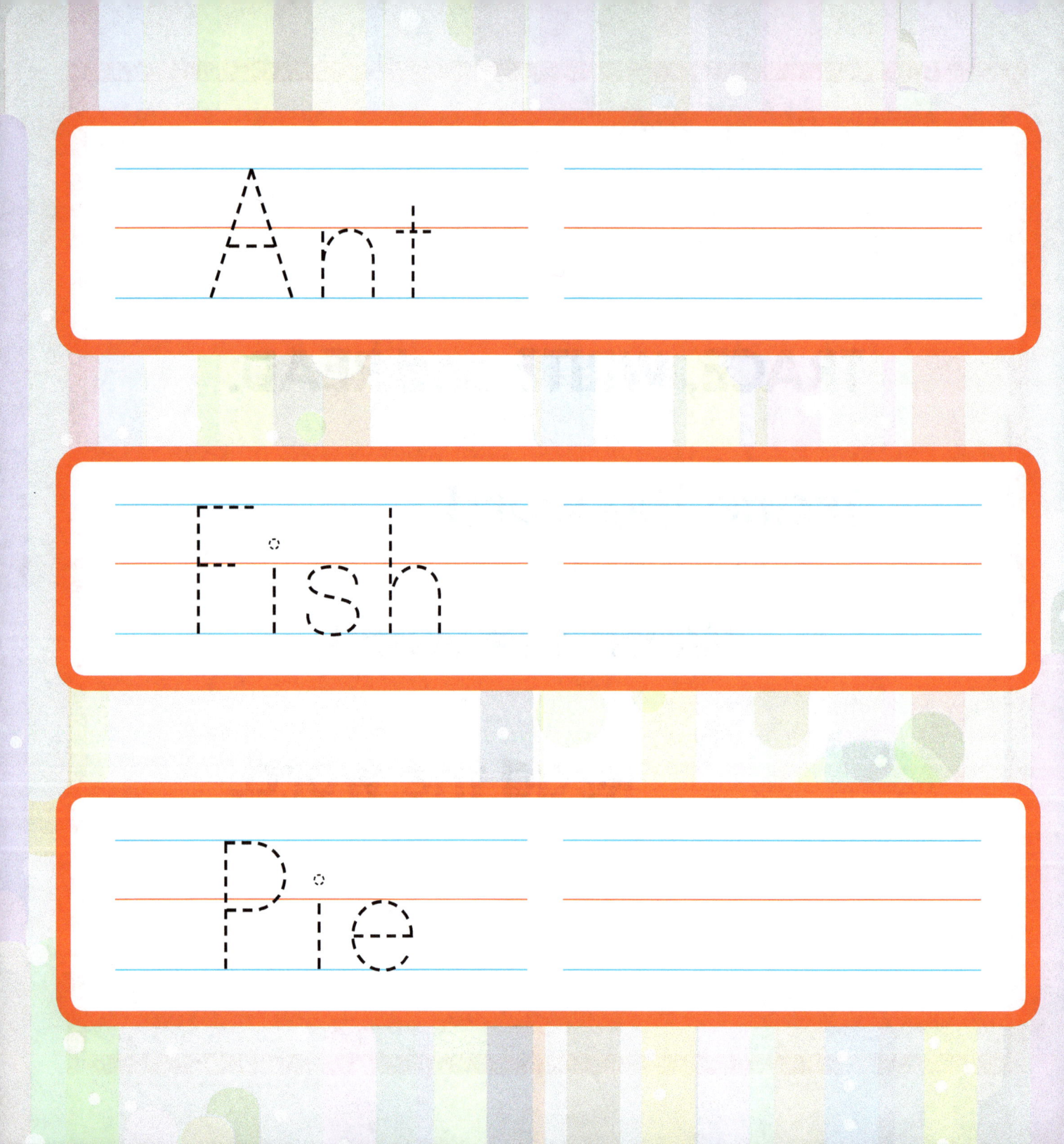

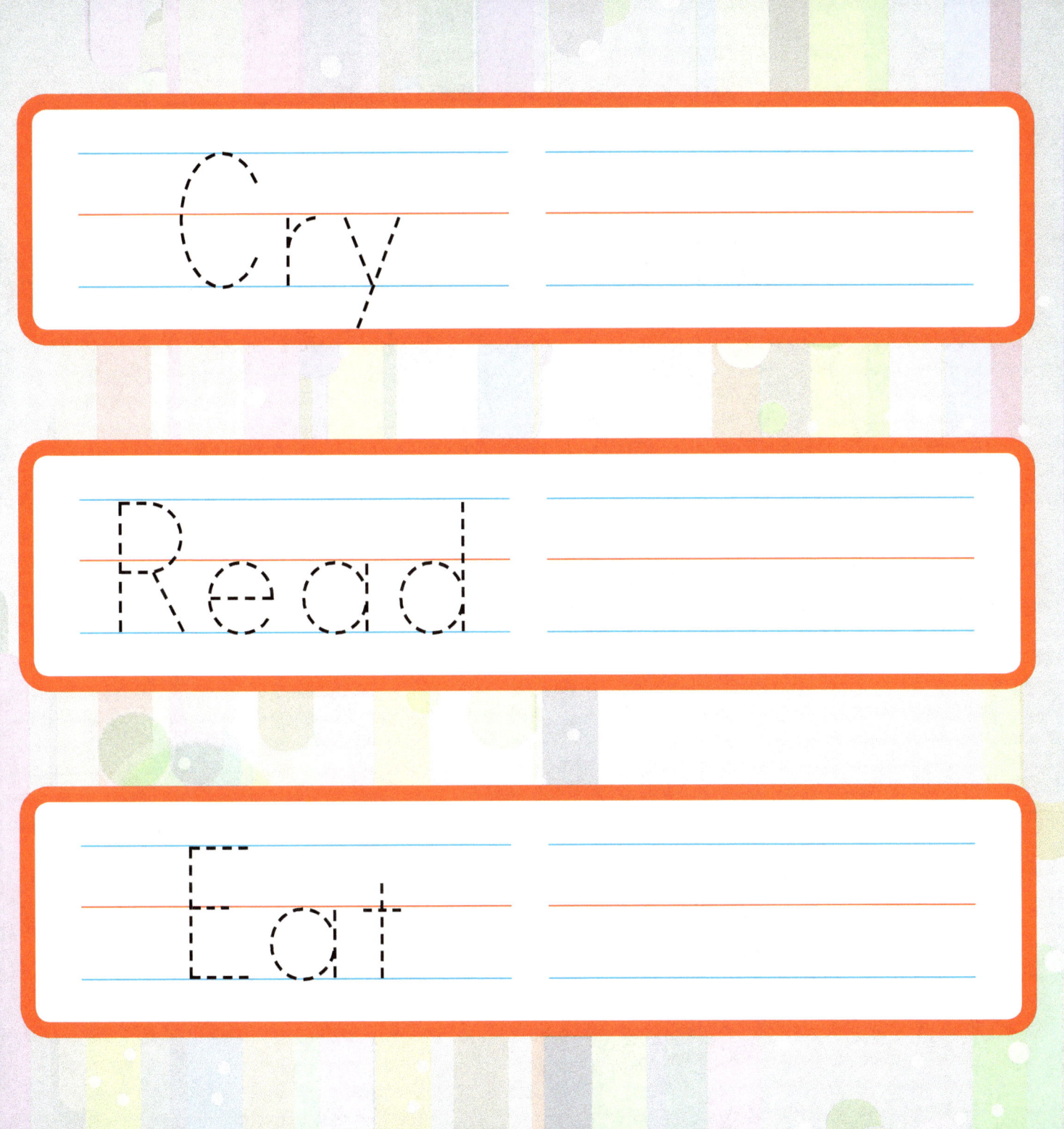

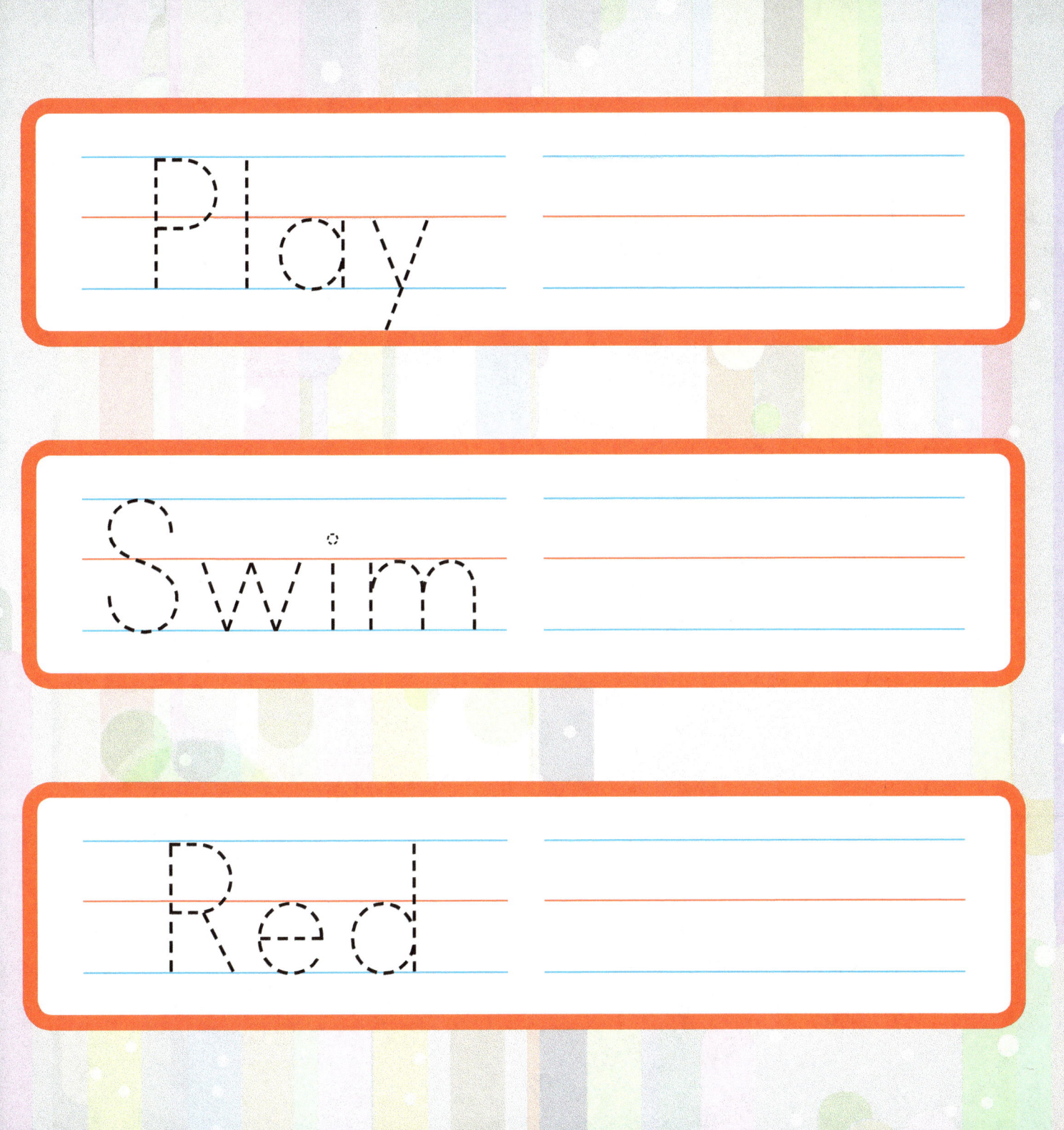

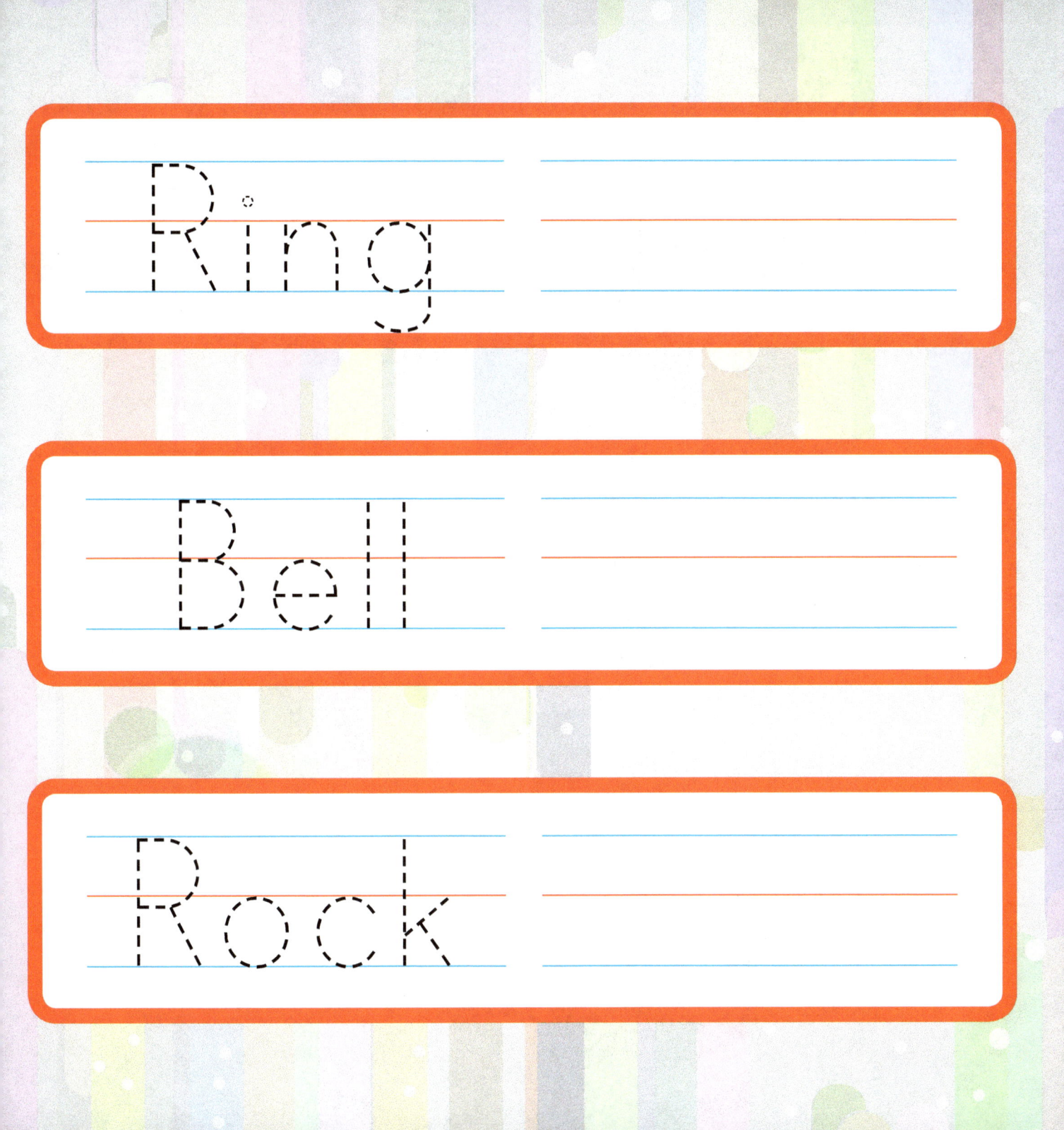

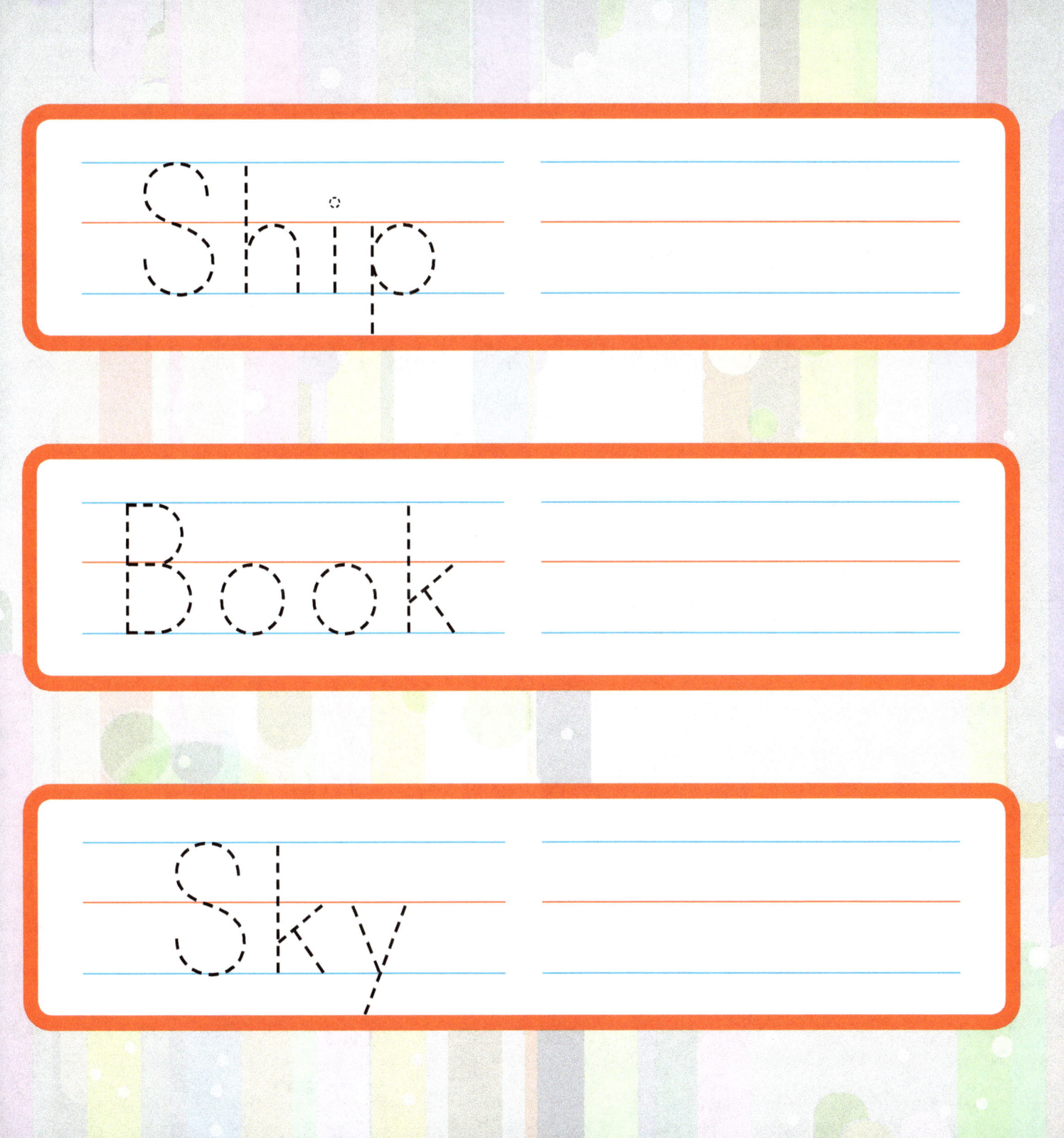

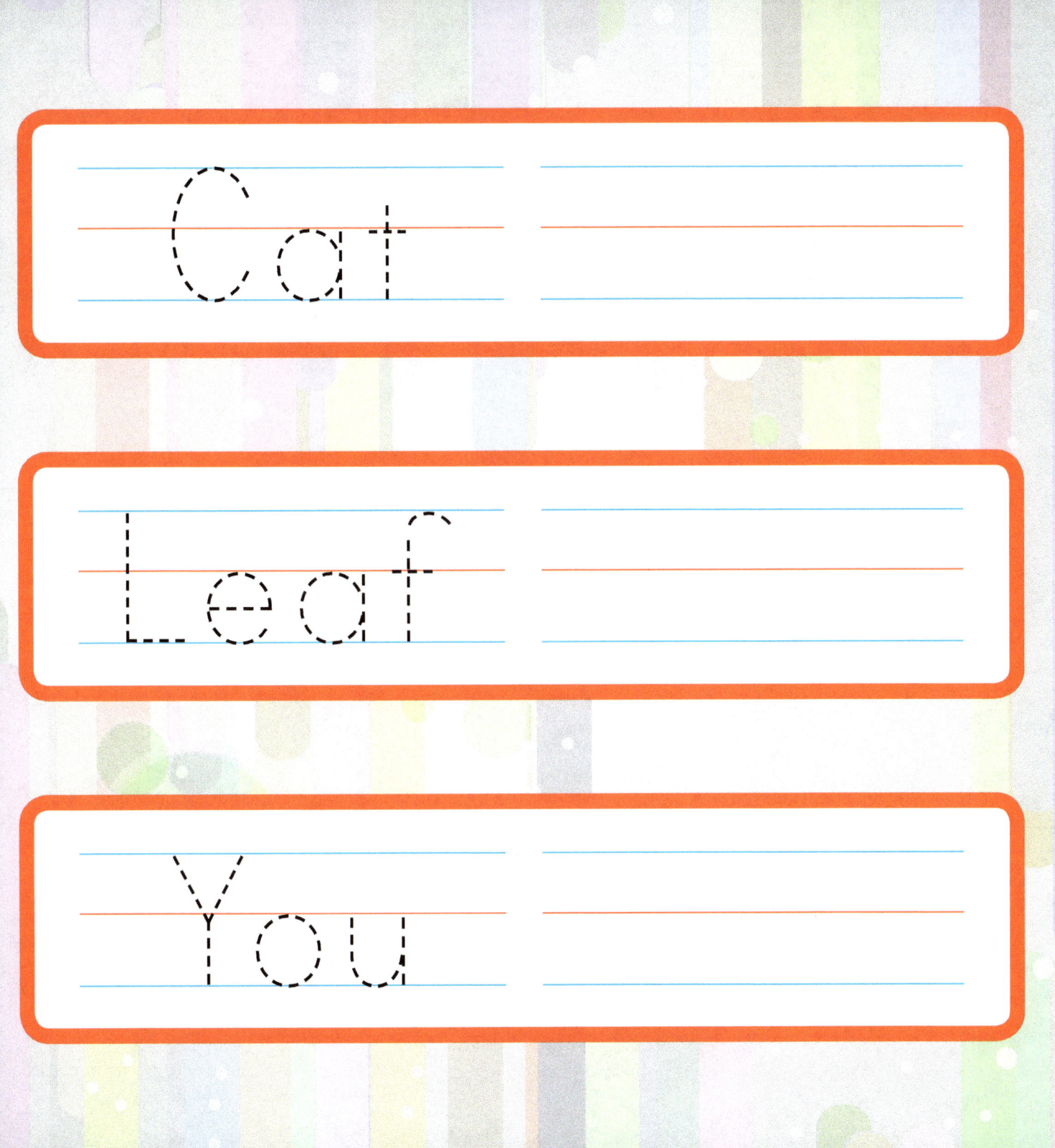

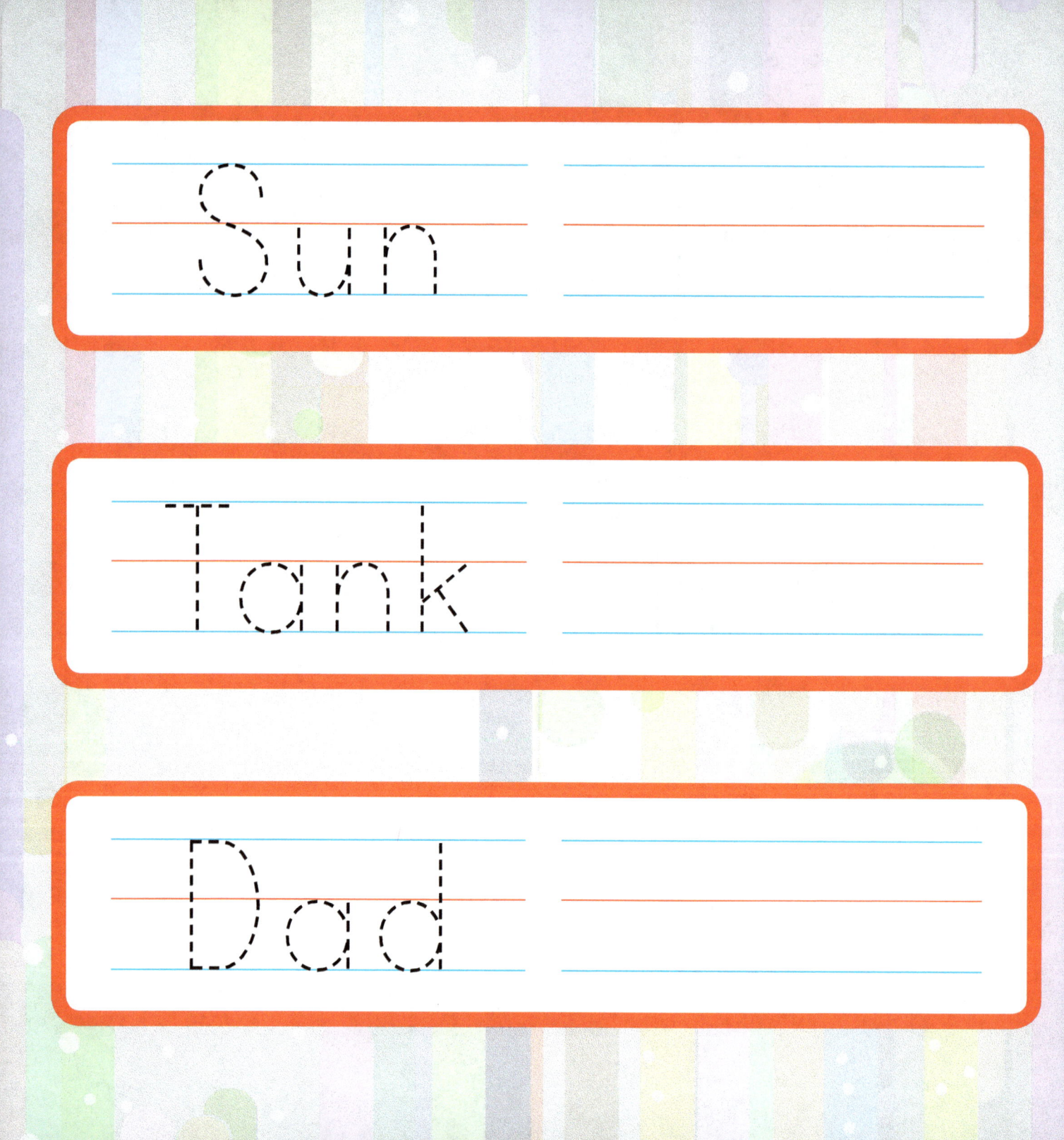

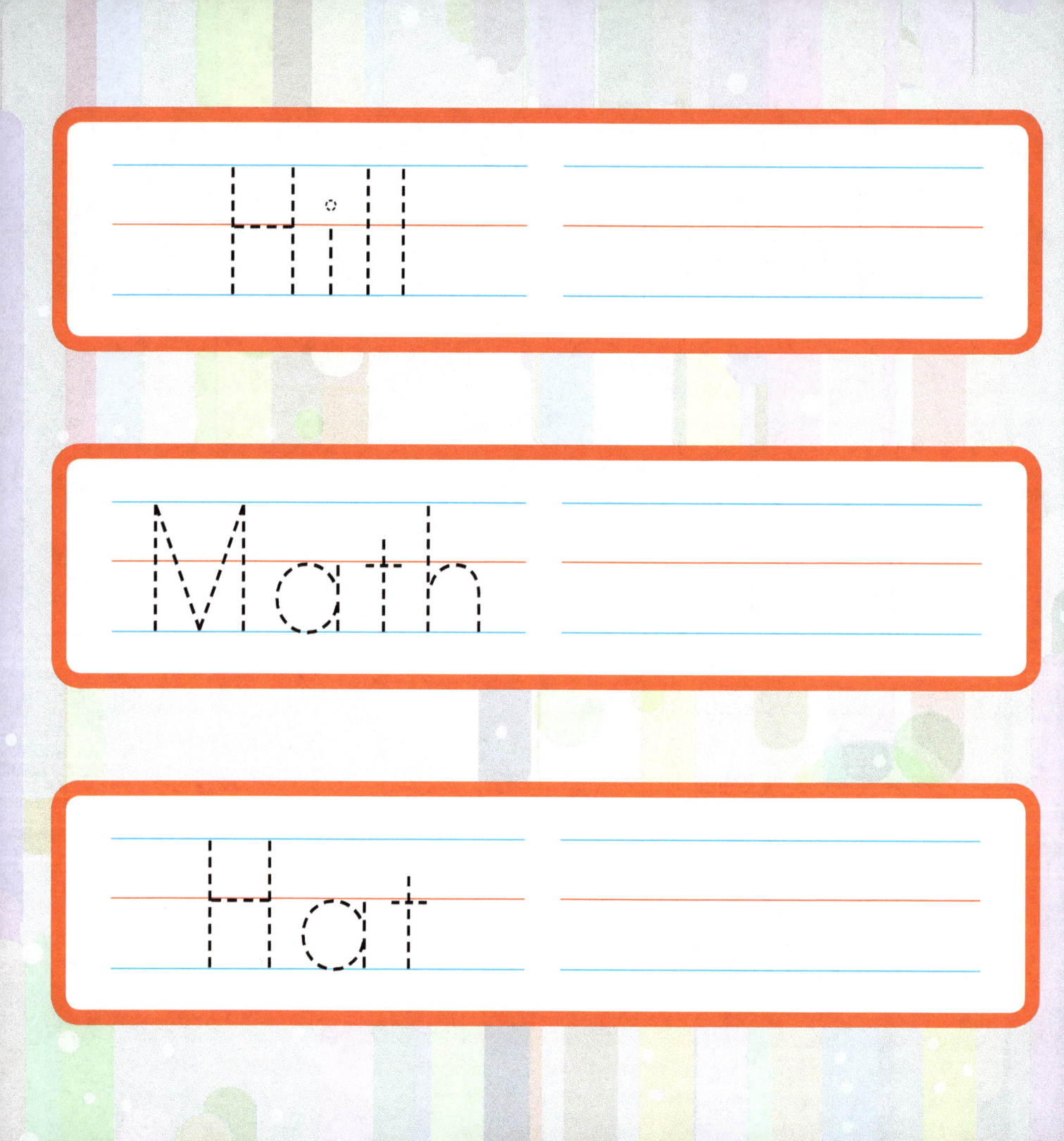

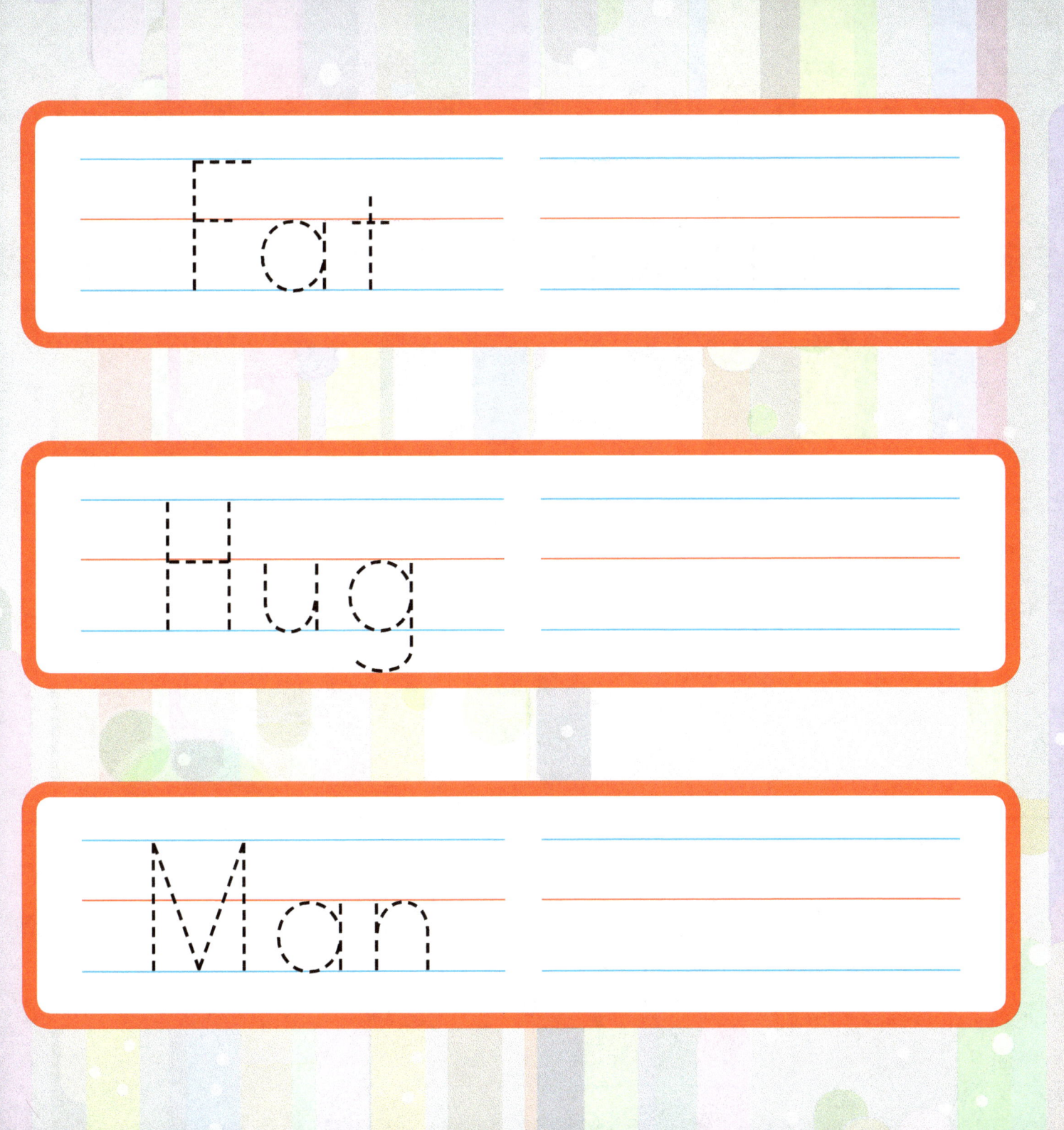

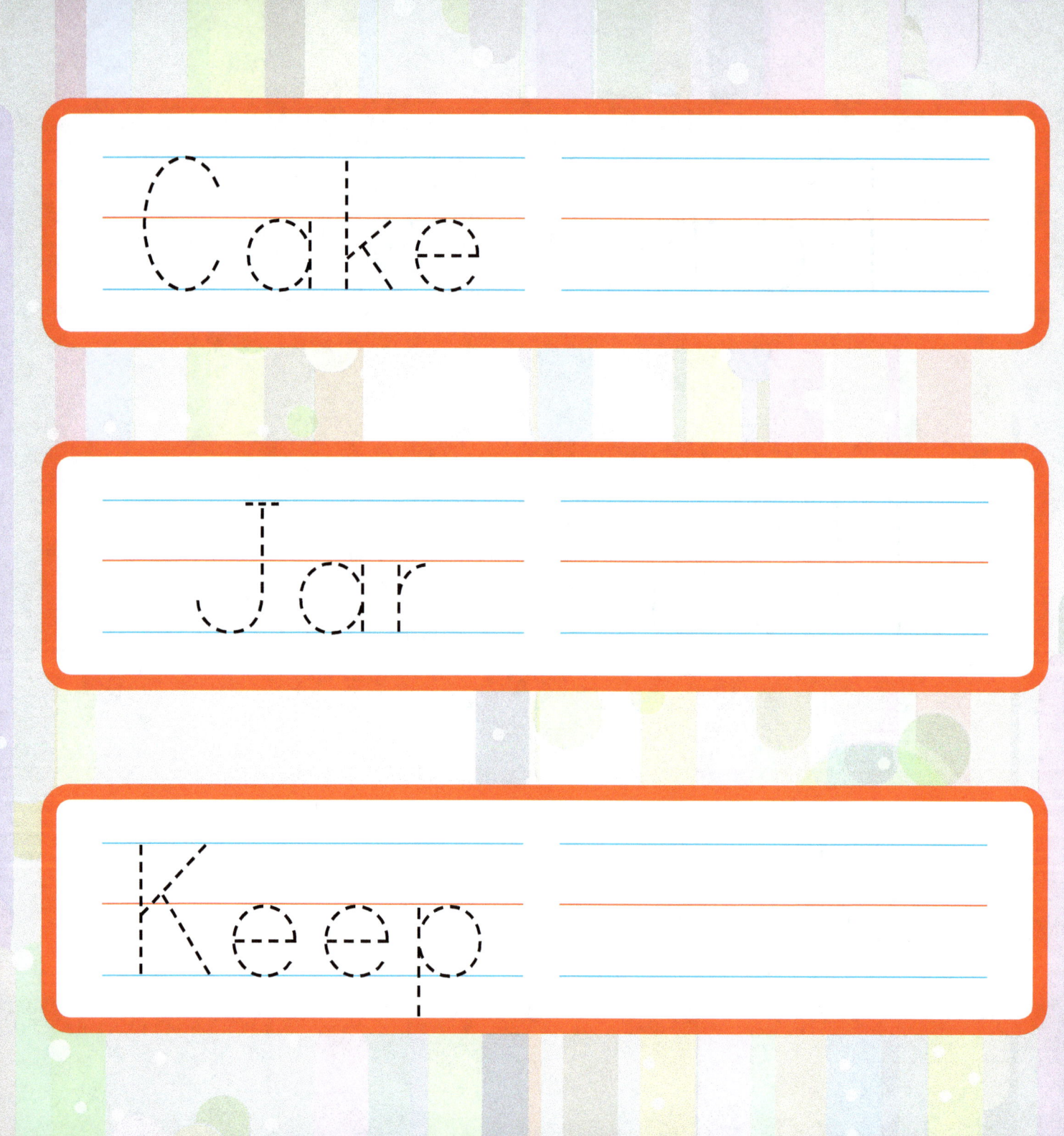

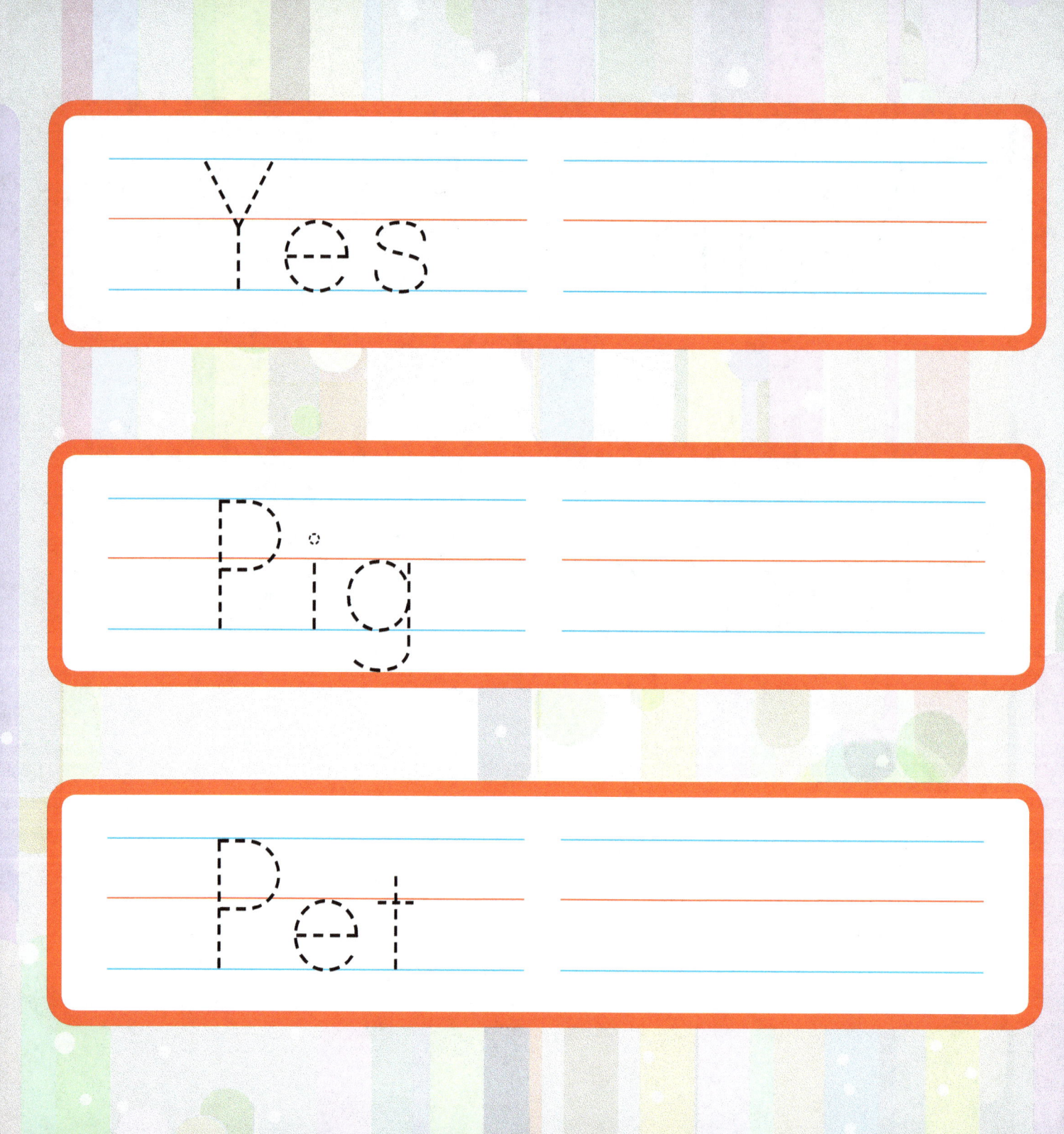

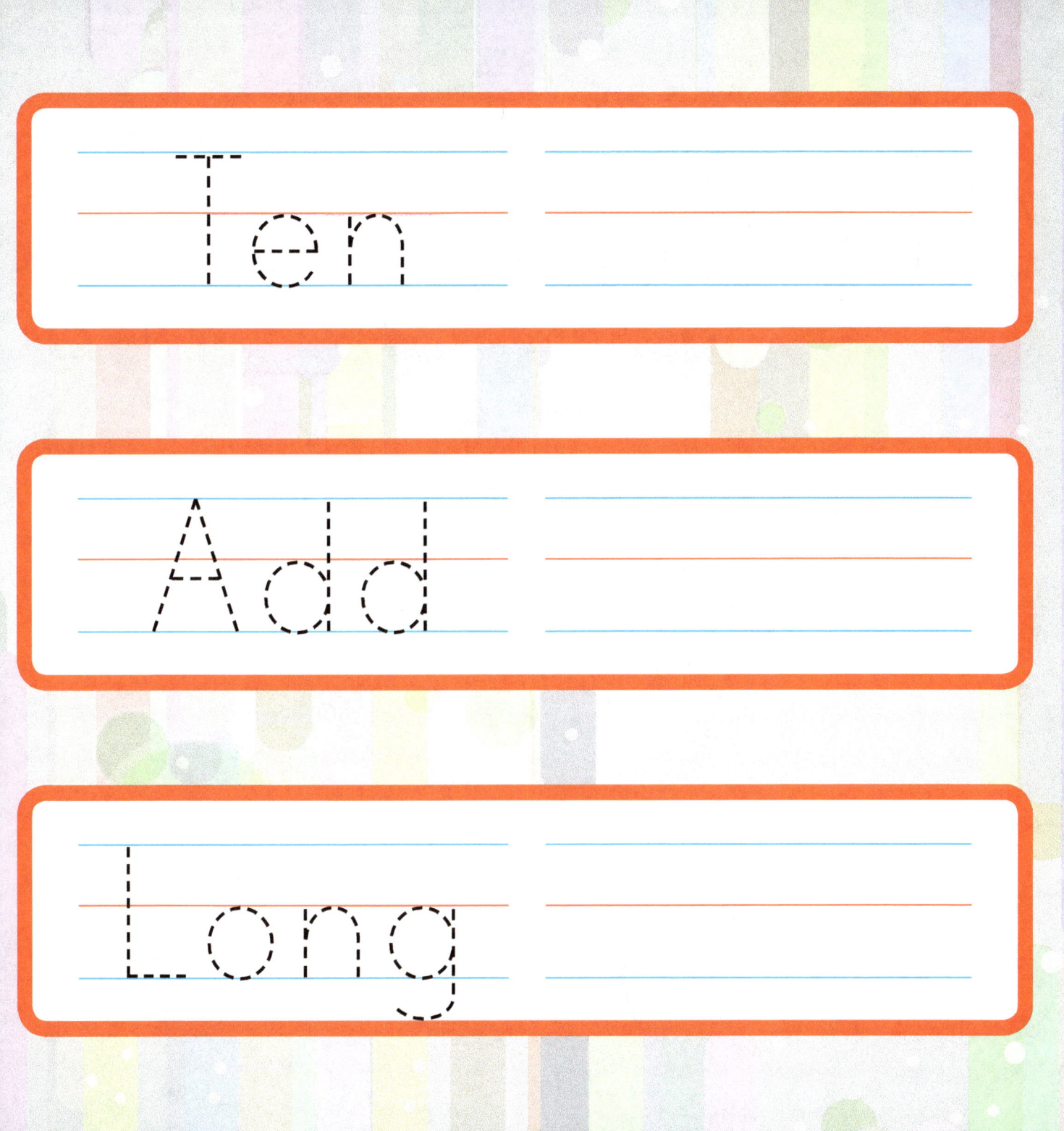

Food

Bag

Baby

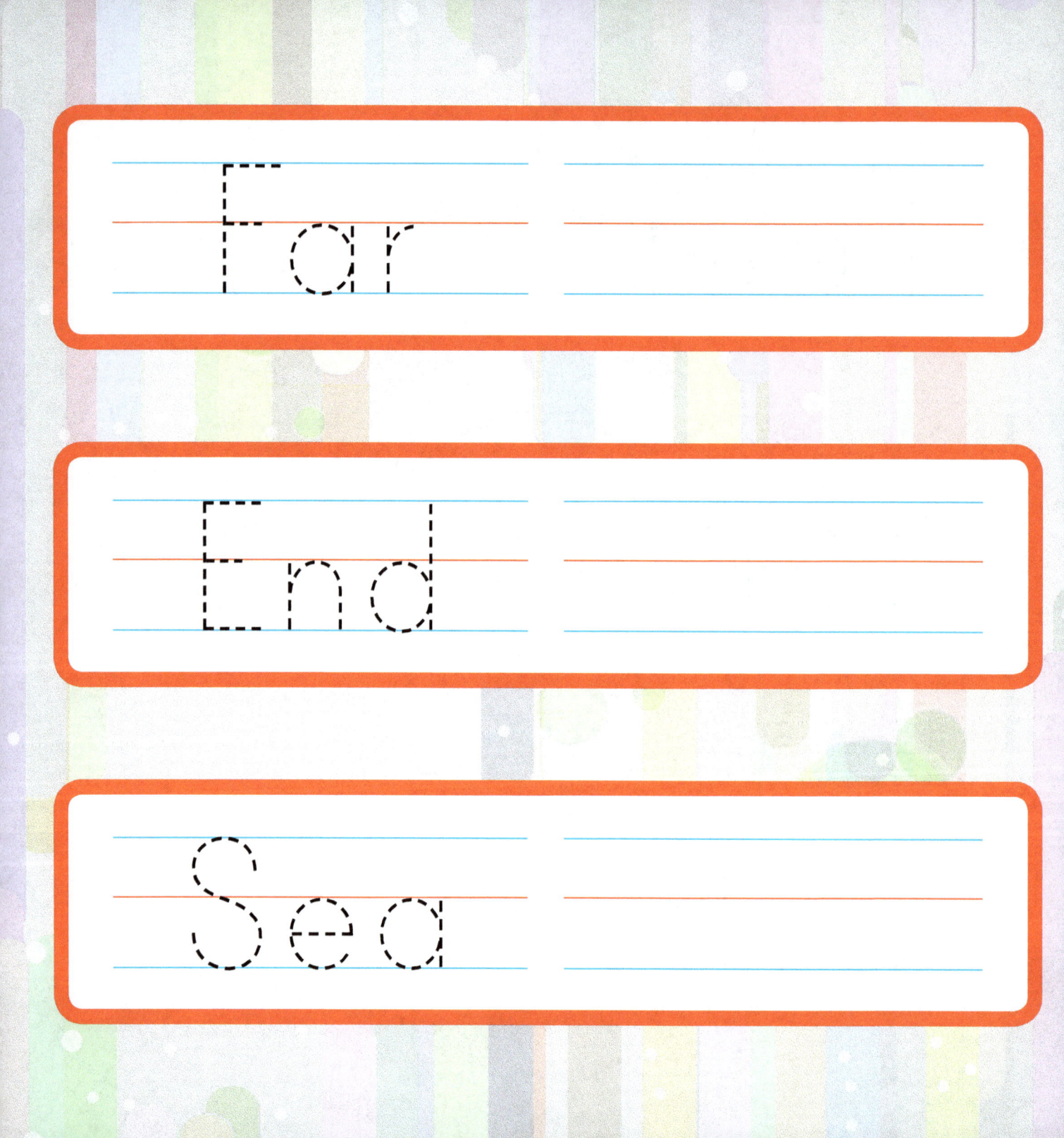

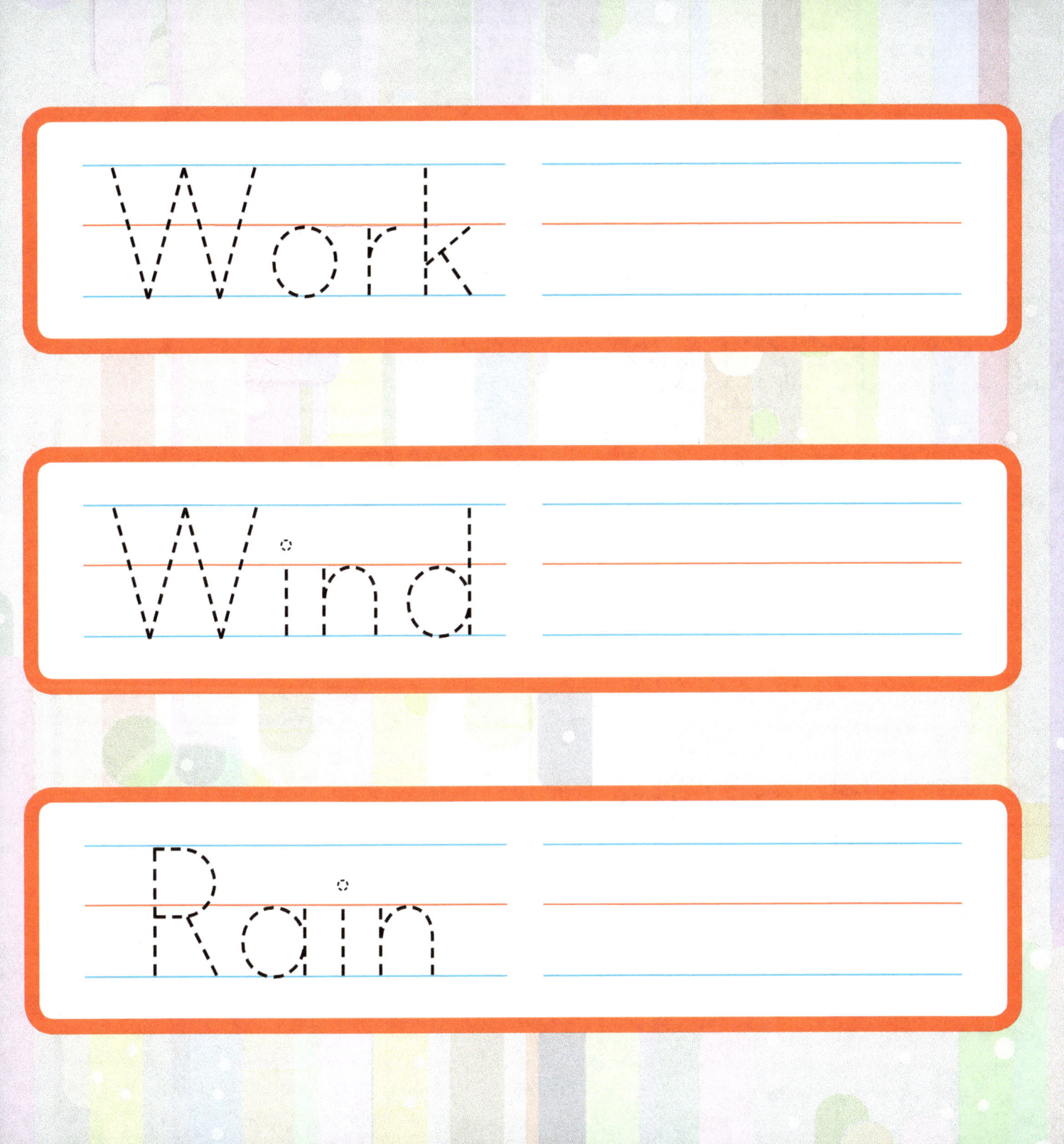

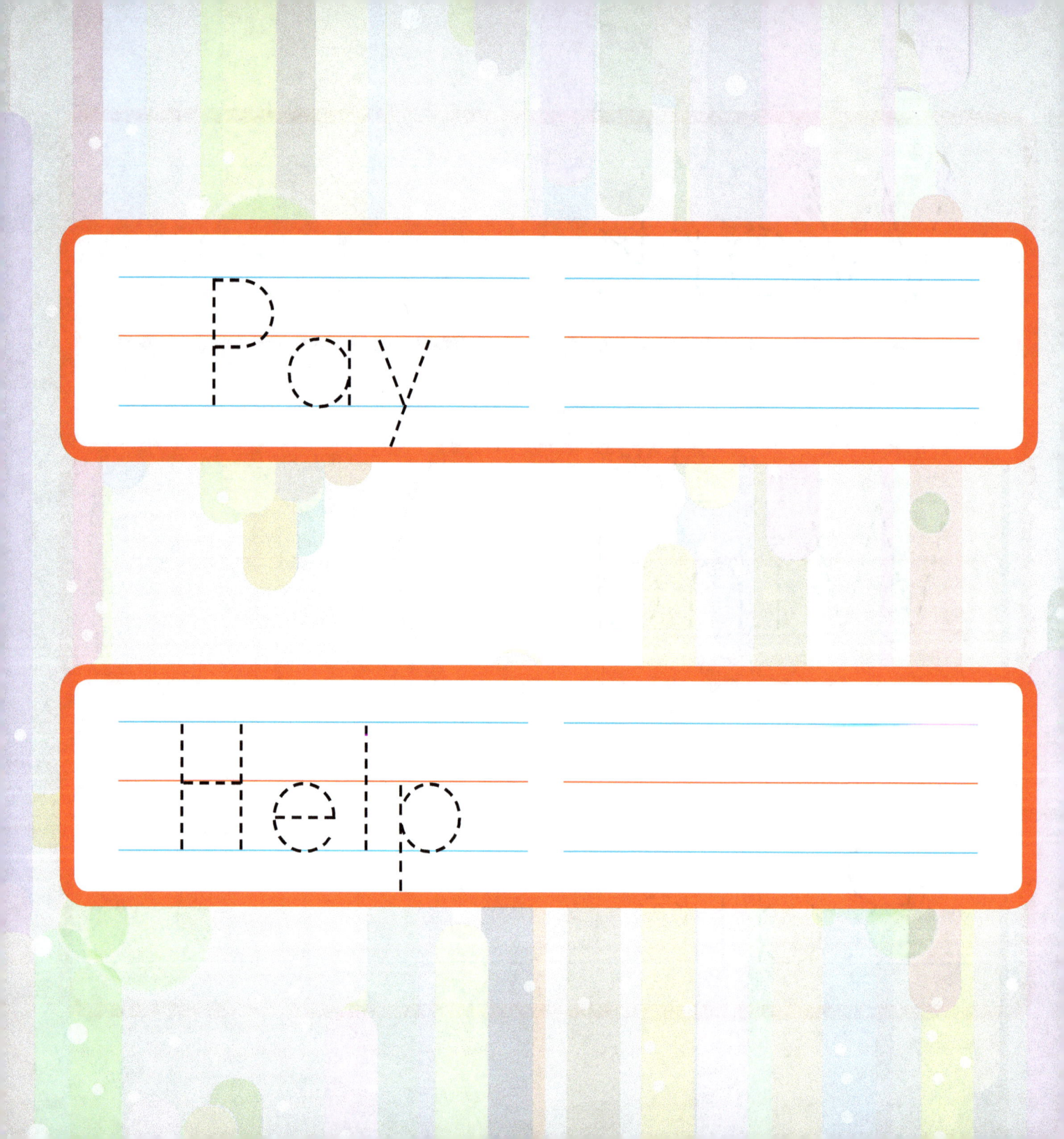

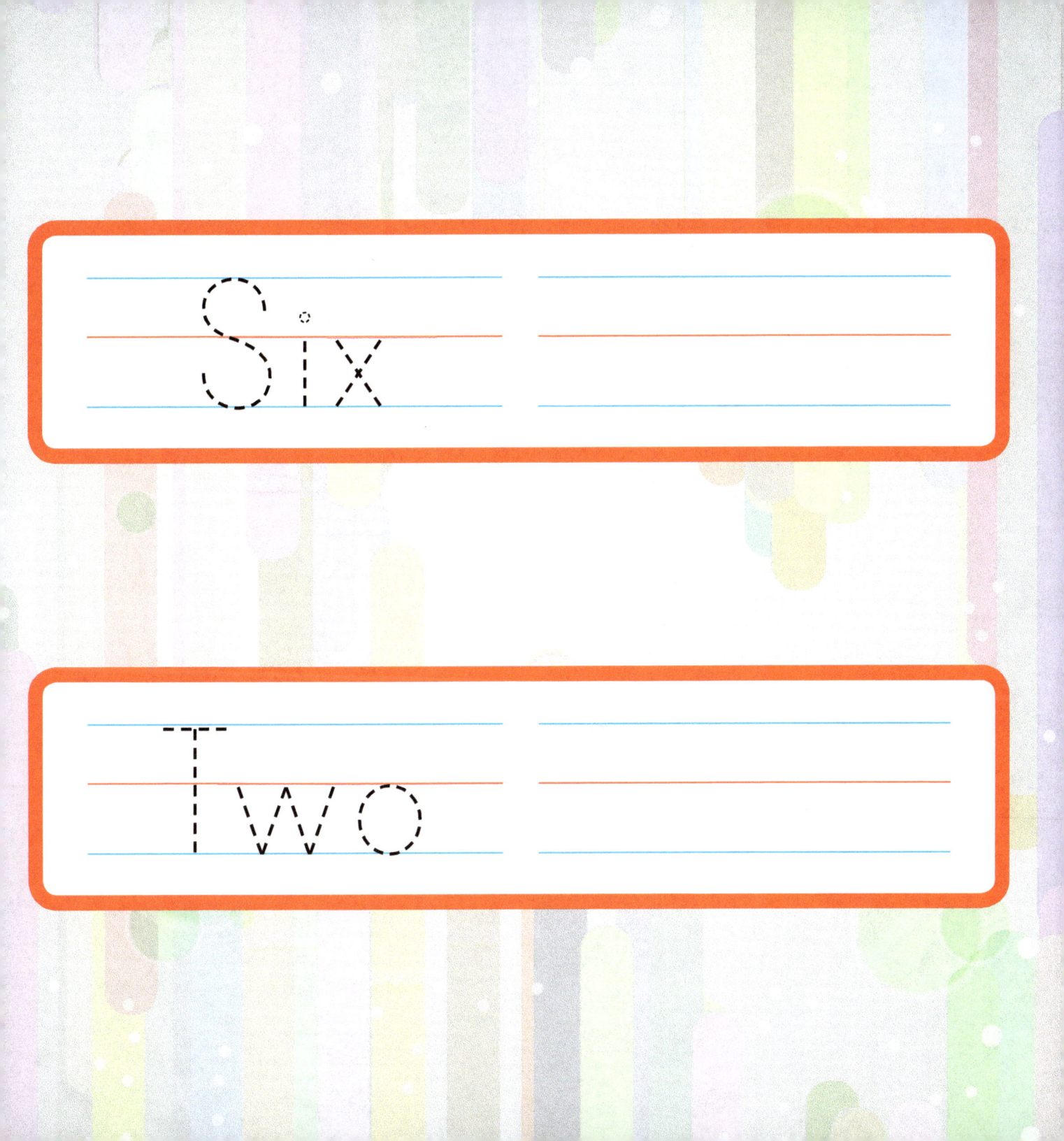

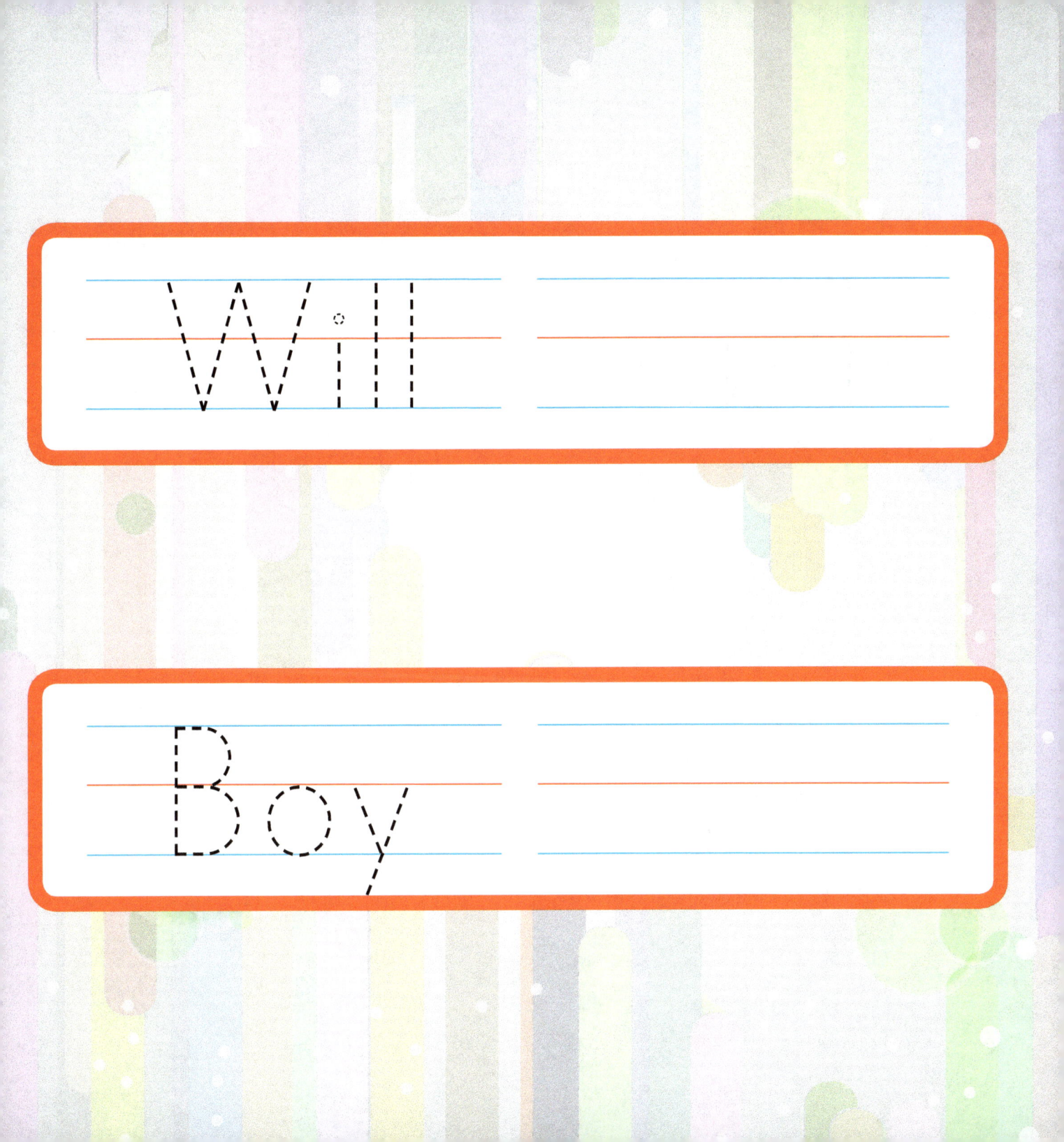

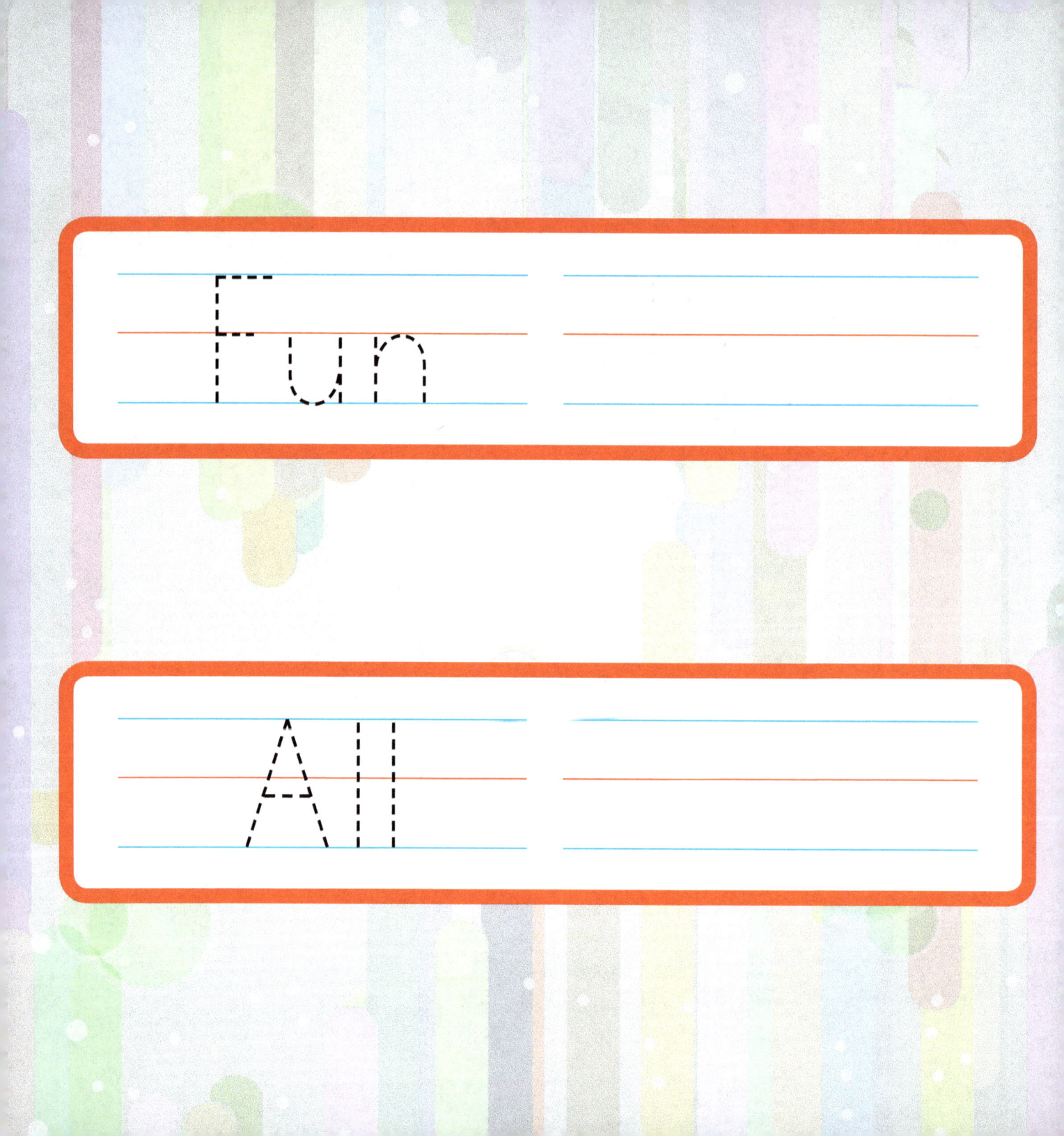

www.ingramcontent.com/pod-product-compliance
Lightning Source LLC
LaVergne TN
LVHW061320060426
835507LV00019B/2246